THE SECRET HISTORY OF CHRISTMAS

Written by Catherine Saunders

First published in Great Britain in 2025 by Wren & Rook

Text copyright © Hodder & Stoughton Limited 2025
Illustrations copyright © Lena Addink 2025
All rights reserved.

The right of Lena Addink to be identified as the illustrator of this Work has been asserted by them in accordance with the Copyright, Designs & Patents Act 1988.

ISBN: 978 1 5263 6807 2

1 3 5 7 9 10 8 6 4 2

Wren & Rook
An imprint of
Hachette Children's Group
Part of Hodder & Stoughton Limited
Carmelite House
50 Victoria Embankment
London EC4Y 0DZ

The authorised representative in the EEA is Hachette Ireland, 8 Castlecourt Centre, Dublin 15, D15 XTP3, Ireland (email: info@hbgi.ie).

An Hachette UK Company
www.hachette.co.uk
www.hachettechildrens.co.uk

Printed and bound in Great Britain by Clays Ltd, Elcograf S.p.A.

CATHERINE SAUNDERS

THE SECRET HISTORY OF CHRISTMAS

TAKE A FESTIVE JOURNEY THROUGH TIME

wren &rook

ILLUSTRATED BY LENA ADDINK

THE SECRET HISTORY OF CHRISTMAS

CONTENTS

INTRODUCTION
Christmas is Coming
7

CHAPTER 1
Christmas Day Coronation
11

CHAPTER 2
A Starry, Starry Christmas
27

CHAPTER 3
Peace at Christmas
41

CHAPTER 4
The Moons of Christmas
57

CHAPTER 5
Super Sporty Christmas
73

CHAPTER 6
Christmas Day Heist
91

CHAPTER 7
The First Christmas?
107

CHAPTER 8
A Christmas Visitor
121

CHAPTER 9
A Christmas Surprise
133

CHAPTER 10
A Christmas Rebellion
145

INTRODUCTION
CHRISTMAS IS COMING

THE SECRET HISTORY OF CHRISTMAS

Christmas is a magical time of year. Twinkly lights, sparkly decorations and bauble-laden trees pop up all over. Catchy Christmas songs blare out wherever you go and you can't seem to get away from Christmas movies on TV, with important messages about kindness, hope and, er, not letting your parents leave you home alone.

Throughout December there are holiday parties and lots of exciting preparations for the big day itself. Christmas Day, 25 December, seems to have its own rules, from the food that gets eaten (and how much of it) to the things that you always do. Most people give gifts. (And receive them, too – woo-hoo!)

You might know the biblical story of Christmas Day already. Baby Jesus

8

CHRISTMAS IS COMING

was born in a humble stable and visited by angels, kings and shepherds. It was there that he was given gifts of gold, frankincense and myrrh by the three wise men.

Many Christians go to church at midnight on Christmas Eve for a service, known as a mass, to celebrate the start of this special birthday. In fact, the word 'Christmas' is a shortened version of 'Christ's Mass'.

However, every year, billions of people from all over the world – from many different cultures and faiths – celebrate, share important traditions and create special moments at Christmas, too.

But did you know that Christmas is a time when other truly AMAZING things have happened over the centuries? From the coronation of kings and the amazing Christmas Day truce to wonderful space missions and incredible inventions, there is a whole secret history of Christmas just waiting to be shared.

THE SECRET HISTORY OF CHRISTMAS

So, get ready to go on a festive journey through history and around the world to uncover some of the most extraordinary things that have happened on and around 25 December. There are incredible stories, fantastic people and amazing moments to discover, as well as lots of impressive facts about the Christmas traditions you already know and love.

CHAPTER 1

CHRISTMAS DAY CORONATION

On 25 December 1066, King William I was crowned King of England (but not Scotland, Wales or Ireland). Now, you might be thinking that Christmas Day was a strange day to choose for a coronation (for a start, wouldn't everyone be busy doing Christmassy things?) but it was actually a very clever move by William. As a Frenchman who had 'won' the English throne in battle, he wanted to send a message to the people in the country that his reign would be a time of peace and hope, not war. So, what better day to do that on than Christmas Day?

THREE (WOULD-BE) KINGS

To appreciate just how brilliant William's idea was, we need to understand a little bit of the history and how a Frenchman came to be king of England in the first place. Nowadays, countries with a king or queen usually know exactly who the next one will be. There will be a very clear line of succession – this means the person who will inherit the role – and it's usually the current monarch's son or daughter. However, back in eleventh-century England, things weren't so clear. When King Edward, known as Edward the Confessor, died on 5 January 1066, he didn't have any surviving children to inherit the throne. His closest relative was his fourteen-year-old great nephew, Edgar the Atheling, who didn't really want to be king – not to mention the fact that he was only a teenager!

CHRISTMAS DAY CORONATION

So, who would be king? (At that time, the idea of having a queen reigning alone would have blown people's minds!) Three people thought that it should be them: King Edward's brother-in-law, Harold Godwinson, an Anglo-Saxon; William of Normandy, a French duke; and Harald Hardrada, a Viking and the King of Norway. They all had strong reasons for claiming the throne of England. Harold thought it should be him because his sister had been queen, plus he had tonnes of money and was from the largest area in England at that time, Wessex. William was a more distant relative, but he claimed that Edward had promised him the throne in 1051. Finally, Harald was a distant relative of King Cnut, a Viking who had ruled England between 1016 and 1035, and he thought that England should have a Viking ruler again. At that time, many people in England were descended from Vikings.

The final decision was made pretty quickly by a group of powerful English nobleman (people from important families who helped the king run the country). They chose Harold Godwinson, and he was crowned on 6 January 1066, just one day after

Edward's death. What a fabulous late Christmas gift, eh?

Harold seemed like an obvious choice: he was a close relative, lived locally and knew all the nobles. However, William and Harald did not accept the nobles' decision and they BOTH decided to invade England (separately) and try to take Harold's place. They were definitely not feeling festive.

BATTLING IT OUT

The new King Harold of England realised that his rivals weren't going to give up without a fight, so he prepared for battle. He assumed that William would get there first (France is closer to England than Norway is, after all) so he waited in the south of England. However, as it turned out, they both took AGES to arrive and it was Harald that reached England first, in September 1066. He invaded the north of England, so King Harold mobilised his army and marched north as quickly as he could. It took them four days to reach the

CHRISTMAS DAY CORONATION

Viking army, but they still managed to catch them by surprise. The two sides fought it out in the Battle of Stamford Bridge ('Harold versus Harald' sounds catchier!) and the English Harold emerged victorious on 25 September 1066. Harald Hardrada didn't survive the battle and what remained of his army went home to Norway.

Unfortunately, King Harold didn't have too long to enjoy his victory, as just three days later, on 28 September 1066, William finally arrived on England's shores with his Norman army. He'd planned to arrive in August, but bad weather had delayed him, which is so typically English that it's a surprise that William didn't change his mind about the whole thing and stay in France. Unlike Harald, William didn't rush into battle straight away, because he wanted to make sure that his army had time to rest after their journey. This also gave King Harold some much-needed time to head back south and gather some fresh troops, before heading even further south to face the Normans. Eventually the two armies met each other at Senlac Hill, just outside Hastings, on 14 October 1066.

THE BATTLE OF HASTINGS

Now, you've probably heard of the Battle of Hastings – maybe you've even learnt about it in school. It's pretty famous, thanks to the Bayeux Tapestry, a famous artwork which tells the story of the battle. They didn't have rolling news channels or YouTube back then, so people had to rely on things like art to find stuff out!

The tapestry included text written in medieval Latin. This scene shows William '… *venit ad pevenesæ*', meaning he '… crossed the sea and came to Pevensey', a small village on the south coast of England.

CHRISTMAS DAY CORONATION

> The Bayeux Tapestry was not made in Bayeux (France). The 68.3-metre long embroidered cloth was most likely created in Canterbury, England, by nuns.

The battle started off pretty well for Harold and his army because they had taken up a great position at the top of Senlac Hill. They formed a strong defensive wall with their shields and waited for the Normans to attack from the bottom of the hill. The Norman archers unleashed their arrows, but gravity was working against them and they couldn't reach the English army. However, William didn't despair because he had a cunning plan. First, he ordered his foot soldiers and cavalry (soldiers on horseback) to attack the hill and then pretend to retreat. Sensing another victory (and probably keen to get home and stop all this battling), Harold's army got completely over-excited and abandoned their strong defensive position to chase the 'retreating' Normans down the hill.

Soon it was utter chaos and the Normans were able to execute the next stage of their plan. As the English army scattered all over the place, the Normans charged up the hill and stole the advantage. Eventually King Harold was killed – according to the Bayeux Tapestry via an arrow in his eye, although no one can be certain that this is what really happened. Tapestries are notoriously unreliable sources of factual information, plus all the English soldiers were dressed identically. Anyway, Harold's death meant that the battle was over. Most of the English army fled, and William had conquered.

However, William still had some work (battling) to do before he could become king. His army had to fight several smaller battles to take control of key towns such as Dover and Winchester, which was England's capital at the time. Unsurprisingly, most English people weren't hugely keen on having a French king. William could see that his job would not be easy, but he wasn't about to turn back now.

CHRISTMAS DAY CORONATION

CHRISTMAS IN 1066

William marched his army towards London because he had decided that this up-and-coming city would be his capital. When he got to London, he declared himself king, becoming known as William I or William the Conqueror. He was determined to try and win as much support as he could from the people of England without further violence, so he planned a grand coronation. He wanted to show his subjects that he deserved to be king and encourage them to follow his new rules. He chose Christmas Day because it was a day when people already felt happy and he thought that this would make them feel more positive towards him.

> Many Roman emperors, such as Charlemagne in 800 CE, had also chosen Christmas Day to be crowned. William hoped that by following their famous examples, it would show people how important he was, too.

Willam's coronation took place in Westminster Abbey, a grand church in London that had been built by Edward the Confessor. Westminster Abbey is still standing today, but only a small part of it is from the original building. Despite William's intentions, his coronation did not turn out to be a particularly joyous occasion – it was a solemn one.

Bishops gave traditional (boring) speeches in English and French and the people inside the Abbey sang special (boring) songs praising the new king. If only he'd had some Christmas carols to liven things up!

There were tensions between the English nobles (Anglo-Saxons) and William's French nobles (Normans). Many English people felt unsettled. They'd had three kings in just one year, there had been several big battles and they were worried about what new laws and customs William might have brought with him from France. The atmosphere was strained, and William made sure that he was protected by many guards. Unfortunately, the guards were so worried about

keeping William safe that when the congregation started singing loudly (and probably quite badly), they misunderstood and thought that they were shouting angrily and getting ready to attack.
The guards panicked and set fire to some nearby buildings, causing most of the congregation to flee. The bishops had to wrap up the coronation pretty quickly after that.

So, William was officially king of England, but his Christmas spirit soon faded. He brought in lots of strict new rules and dealt harshly with anyone who opposed him. Over the years, quite a few different groups tried to rebel against William, including more Vikings. However, one of his main threats came from Edgar the Atheling (remember him?) who had decided that he would like to be king after all. He had support from Denmark and Scotland, but William crushed Edgar's rebellion and punished anyone who had supported him. Talk about dampening the Christmas spirit.

William was king of England for twenty-one years, but despite his Christmas coronation, his reign was anything but festive. He limited people's freedom, especially women, and had huge, imposing castles built (including the famous Tower of London) to keep his nobleman safe and show the Anglo-Saxons that the Normans were there to stay.

Next time you pull a cracker and put a paper crown on, just think – for one king, it was a real one!

STOCKING FILLER FACTS

CHRISTMAS DINNER

No one knows what William the Conqueror ate for his Christmas dinner, but food on Christmas Day is definitely a big deal.

Take a look at some Christmas dinners from around the world. Some of them take days to prepare (and nearly as long to eat).

TURKEY AND ALL THE TRIMMINGS

In the UK especially, the traditional Christmas dinner is roast turkey with so many extras that they can barely fit on your plate. These include roast potatoes, stuffing, tiny sausages wrapped in bacon, gravy and cranberry sauce, plus a whole lot of veg too, including Brussels sprouts – which many people HATE and others love.

CHRISTMAS BARBECUE

People who live in hot countries, such as Australia, don't always want a massive roast dinner on Christmas Day. In fact, many families in the southern hemisphere have a traditional festive barbecue on the beach!

WE FISH YOU A MERRY CHRISTMAS

In many countries, fish is traditionally served as part of Christmas dinner, from salted cod in Portugal and Mexico to herring and smoked salmon in Sweden. On Christmas Eve in Italy, families enjoy *Festa dei Sette Pesci* (the Feast of the Seven Fish), which, as the name suggests, involves eating SEVEN different types of fish and seafood.

THE TWELVE COURSES OF CHRISTMAS

In Poland, Lithuania and Ukraine on Christmas Eve, it's usual to eat TWELVE different courses, including lots of fish. Often, the meal only starts when the first star appears in the night sky.

CHRISTMAS DAY CORONATION

CHRISTMAS IN JANUARY

In Ethiopia, thanks to their different calendar, Christmas Day, known as *Ganna* or *Genna*, falls on 7 January. On this day, Ethiopian families eat a spicy chicken stew called *doro wat* and drink a special type of coffee.

KENTUCKY FRIED CHRISTMAS

Christmas Day is not a public holiday in Japan, but thanks to an advertising campaign in the 1970s it's now traditional for many families to order KFC on Christmas Day. The queues are so massive that many people pre-order their chicken weeks before.

CHAPTER 2

A STARRY, STARRY CHRISTMAS

On 25 December 2021, NASA (the USA's National Aeronautics and Space Administration), CSA (the Canadian Space Agency) and ESA (the European Space Agency) joined forces to launch the enormous and extremely powerful James Webb Space Telescope into space. It was on an ambitious mission to orbit the Sun and see deeper into the universe than anything else before.

Christmas Day 2021 must have been a very busy one for the team of experts in charge of the launch, but not because of having to wrap presents, play lots of charades or even cook an elaborate meal. Instead, they had to ensure that the launch went PERFECTLY . . . because if it didn't, thirty years of hard work and roughly $10 billion would have been wasted. Now that would have been a very un-merry Christmas!

SEEING STARS

For a lot of people, Christmas Day is a day off. Though some people, such as those who work in healthcare, the emergency services or hospitality, to name a few, do have to work. They do an amazing job, but it could be quite hard for them and their families. Just like these special people, the dedicated team in charge of launching the James Webb Space Telescope were prepared to miss one Christmas for something very important.

Named after a former head of NASA, the James Webb Space Telescope's mission was to try and see light from the oldest stars in the universe. These stars are believed to be more than 13.5 billion years old, and the telescope would have to travel 1.5 million km from Earth to try and detect light from them. Like looking at the twinkling lights of a Christmas tree from very, very, very far away!

TIME TRAVEL IS POSSIBLE (SORT OF)!

You probably have a bunch of questions about how we can possibly see light from stars that have been around for so long and are so far away. You're right to wonder but be warned: the answers may make your brain hurt a little because they kind of involve time travel and some MASSIVE numbers. OK, here goes . . .

Space is so HUGE that distance isn't usually measured in kilometres or miles, but in light years. A light year is the distance that light travels in one (Earth) year, which roughly equals about 9 trillion kilometres. A trillion has twelve zeros, so you can imagine that if we used kilometres to measure distances in space, we'd soon get overwhelmed by zeros and probably run out of room to write them down. That's why we use light years to measure the huge distances in space.

So far so good, but you're probably asking: what about the time travel part?

Well, light travels at 300,000 km per second, which is super fast, but stars are INCREDIBLY FAR AWAY. For example, the closest star to Earth is the Sun, which is more than 150 million km away. It takes about 8.3 minutes for light from the Sun to reach Earth, which means that what we're really seeing is how the Sun looked 8.3 minutes ago. (That also means that it would also take us 8.3 minutes to notice if the Sun ever disappeared . . .) The next closest star to Earth, Proxima Centauri, is much further away, about 4.3 light years. So that means when we see light from Proxima Centauri, it's taken so long to reach us that we're actually seeing light from 4.3 years ago.

A STARRY, STARRY CHRISTMAS

Now the time travel idea is starting to make sense, right? Let's take it a giant leap further then. The 'observable universe' is about 93 billion light years in diameter (this is the part of the universe we know about and have the technology to observe, but there's probably way more that we don't know about and can't see yet). So, as the universe is so massive, some stars must be really, really, really far away. Therefore, the light we see from these stars was actually produced hundreds, thousands, even billions of years ago – it has just taken an incredibly long time to get to us. And it's the light from the most far-off stars of all, formed billions of years ago when the universe began, that the James Webb Space Telescope (let's call it the JWST for short from now on) was built to detect.

HOW THE JWST WORKS

Because they're so old and so far away, we know very little about the secrets of the first stars. However, scientists use what they do know about other stars (the younger ones that are closer to

THE SECRET HISTORY OF CHRISTMAS

Earth) to form clever theories and ideas about how these ancient stars formed, what they're made of and what that all means for our universe. They wanted the JWST to help them explore the furthest parts of the universe and find out if their theories were correct. That's a lot of work for a Christmas Day!

Telescopes can see objects that are far away by using mirrors to gather and reflect light, so the bigger the mirror, the more light the telescope can gather. In order to see light that is sooooooo far away, the JWST had to be the largest and most powerful telescope ever built. Its main mirror is 6.5 metres in diameter and made up of eighteen golden hexagonal segments that were designed to reflect a special kind of light – infrared – that the human eye cannot see.

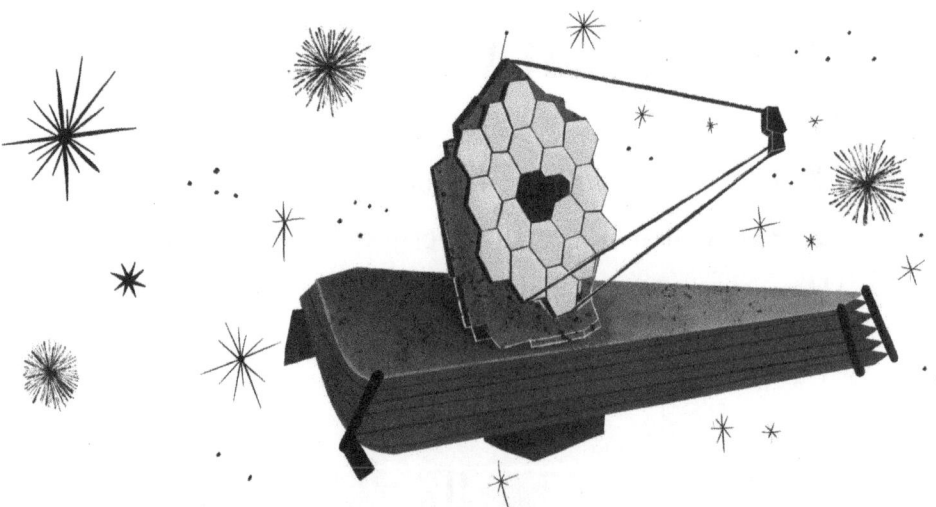

A STARRY, STARRY CHRISTMAS

One of the lead scientists on the project is Dr Jane Rigby. For the work she does overseeing the JWST, she was awarded the Presidential Medal of Freedom by Joe Biden in May 2024.

Due to its enormous mirror and other equipment that helps it to function, the whole JWST covers an area about the size of a tennis court, which means that launching it into space was not easy. The clever scientists made the JWST foldable so that it would fit inside a rocket. In many ways it was a bit like trying to wrap a really tricky, enormous, super-expensive Christmas present. The plan was to launch the rocket and then, at a specified point, the JWST would unpack itself, slowly unfurl to its full size and begin its mission.

LIFT OFF

The scientists had calculated that there were 344 potential 'single-point failures' or moments when, if things didn't happen exactly as planned, JWST's mission would fail. So you can probably understand why the team were so nervous about the launch that everyone was prepared to give up their usual Christmas Day celebrations to make sure that it all went perfectly.

The experts had to check and re-check that everything was working properly on the telescope and then plan exactly what the JWST would do in space and precisely when it would happen. There was absolutely no room for error. There were also logistical problems to solve too, such as the fact that the JWST had been built in California, USA, but would be launched from French Guiana, a French territory located in South America. The solution was to transport the JWST 9,300 km, very carefully, by ship.

> Rocket launch sites are often near the equator because the Earth spins faster there (because that's where its circumference is widest), which gives the rockets an extra boost as they blast off into space.

The JWST was packed into a specially made 'suitcase' known as the Space Telescope Transporter for Air, Road and Sea (or STTARS for short) to protect it and keep it a hundred per cent clean. It spent sixteen days at sea (the ship sailed very slowly and avoided any rough seas) before arriving safely in French Guiana on 12 October 2021. After a lot more checks, tests, plans and calculations, the JWST was finally ready to go and was carefully placed inside the nose of an Ariane 5 rocket (chosen for its reliability) on the launch pad on 23 December. The launch was officially set for 24 December 2021, Christmas Eve, but it was postponed for a day due to windy weather.

Finally, on 25 December 2021, the JWST was ready for launch and, just like excited kids and adults on

Christmas Day, the launch team got up early. By 9.20 a.m. local time, while most people were still opening their presents, the Ariane 5 rocket had blasted off into space.

A CHRISTMAS MIRACLE

Amazingly, everything seemed to go to plan, with the JWST transmitting data back to Earth within just five minutes. After twenty-seven minutes, the Ariane 5 rocket separated from the telescope, as planned, and the JWST's solar array unfolded to begin providing power. Then, on 26 December, while most people were eating leftovers in their pyjamas and playing with their Christmas presents, the JWST deployed its antennas, enabling it to send data back to Earth twice a day.

By 27 December, when most people shudder at even the idea of a short walk, the JWST had travelled beyond the Moon's orbit, and on 31 December, it unfurled its enormous sunshield. Shaped a bit like a kite, the sunshield would help keep the telescope cool, and its successful deployment in space was crucial. Everything was going according to plan, and in early January 2022, the JWST began to unfold and align its mirrors, a process that took around four months to complete. On 24 January, the JWST reached its final orbit, a spot 1.5 million km away known as L2, where it can stay in line with the Earth as it moves around the Sun.

Finally, on 11 July 2022, the first colour images from the JWST were shown to the world, revealing hidden parts of the universe that had never been captured before. The mission was undoubtedly a success, down to clever scientists, incredible technology and meticulous planning. But maybe launching on Christmas Day added a bit of extra magic too . . .

STOCKING FILLER FACTS

CHRISTMAS PUDDING

A bit like a voracious black hole gobbling up stars and planets, many people have a bit too much to eat over Christmas. From traditional cakes to cute festive-themed biscuits, it's a time full of tempting treats. Here are some of the yummiest (maybe) festive sweet things.

FESTIVE FRUITCAKE

Whether you love it or hate it, you'll find Christmas fruitcake on many festive tables around the world. It's been a tradition since Roman times and they can be made months in advance.

MINCE PIES

You might think that mince pies sound like they should be made of meat, and that's because at one time they were! In the Middle Ages, they were filled with minced meat and fruit.

Over the years, people stopped adding the meat, but the name stuck.

SURPRISE PUDDING

In Denmark, the main Christmas dessert is *risalamande*, a rice pudding topped with cherry sauce. Hidden inside is one whole almond, and whoever finds it gets a present.

CAKE FOR BREAKFAST?

In the Philippines, many people eat a special salty-and-sweet rice flour cake called *bibingka* after attending Midnight Mass on Christmas Eve. It has coconut milk, butter and eggs and is often then topped with cheese, salted duck egg and grated coconut.

VIKING/FRENCH FUSION

Bûche de Noël is a French log-shaped Christmas cake inspired by the actual logs Vikings used to burn during their Yule winter festival. Usually chocolate flavoured, it is decorated with chocolate icing to represent tree bark and icing sugar to look like snow.

CHAPTER 3

PEACE AT CHRISTMAS

On 25 December 1914, soldiers paused fighting in the First World War for one day (this is known as a truce) to celebrate Christmas. It was an extraordinary moment. The opposing sides put down their guns, set aside their different views and decided to enjoy the festivities together instead.

By this time, the First World War had been going on for nearly five months with millions of casualties. Most of the soldiers who were fighting in the war were far from home, tired, hungry and wondering if they would ever see the people they loved again. Being away from their families at Christmas must have been so difficult but, incredibly, the soldiers managed to find some Christmas spirit during those dark times.

'IT'LL BE OVER BY CHRISTMAS!'

When the First World War started on 28 July 1914, most people thought it would be over very quickly. Everyone was hopeful that things could be sorted out by Christmas, but they weren't. In fact, the war lasted until 11 November 1918. It is often called the Great War – not because it was great (far from it) – but because it affected so many people all over the world. To really understand how special that Christmas 1914 truce was, we need to know a bit more about how and why the war began and what it was like for the soldiers who fought in it.

PEACE AT CHRISTMAS

ALLIANCES AND EMPIRES

In the early twentieth century, the world looked a bit different to how it is today. Not just because they didn't have the awesome technology we have or because they dressed a bit differently – many countries had different names and were ruled in totally different ways. In Europe, a few powerful nations had built empires by forcibly taking over other countries (often far away, on different continents), against their will. They made them obey their laws and took their natural resources. Great Britain, Germany, Russia and Austria-Hungary, for example, had all built large empires and were keen to keep making them bigger, whether other countries wanted that or not. They built huge armies and navies to protect themselves and to help expand their empires, and they also worried about the size of each other's empires. This created tensions and rivalries, especially in Europe, so some countries made alliances (a bit like friendships, but for countries) and promised to support and defend each other if they ever needed to.

The two main alliances in Europe were the Triple Entente, which was between Great Britain, France and Russia, and the Triple Alliance, which was between Germany, Austria–Hungary and Italy. By 1914, tensions were high as some nations wanted bigger empires and others wanted the freedom to rule themselves. In the end all it took was one fateful moment to spark a war.

A CHAIN OF EVENTS

On 28 June 1914, a young Bosnian Serb named Gavrilo Princip killed Archduke Franz Ferdinand, the heir to the Austro-Hungarian throne, and his wife, Sophie, because he believed that Serbia should rule Bosnia, not Austria-Hungary. Princip's actions meant that Austria–Hungary declared war on Serbia on 28 July. Then, Russia's alliance with Serbia meant that Russia declared war on Austria-Hungary, so, of course, Germany had to declare war on Russia because of their alliance with Austria–Hungary. (It's all a bit complicated . . .)

PEACE AT CHRISTMAS

Instead of heading east to fight Russia, in a surprise move the German army headed west instead, hoping to defeat France before they could join the war and help their ally Russia. It was a clever idea, but it absolutely did not work. Great Britain was not involved at this point. The government there hoped that the fighting would end soon and they would be able to stay out of it completely. However, when Germany invaded Belgium (it's on the way to France, after all), Britain had to act. Belgium was a neutral country (which means that it wasn't taking sides) but Britain had promised to protect it if needed – which it now did.

So, on 4 August 1914, the British government demanded that Germany withdraw from Belgium or Great Britain would declare war. Germany ignored the ultimatum and Great Britain entered the First World War. With so many strong armies involved, people hoped that it would all be over quickly, but the opposite happened.

TRENCH WARFARE

As the different armies moved across Europe to face each other, everyone wanted to win the war, but they were even more focused on making sure that they didn't lose it. On the Western Front – the battlegrounds of western Europe, mostly in France and Belgium – the soldiers dug long ditches, known as trenches, opposite each other and spent all day and most of the night firing machine guns and other powerful artillery back and forth to defend their positions. Although they damaged each other's trenches and killed many soldiers on both sides, no one made much progress. The war became a stalemate (no one was able to win).

The trenches on the Western Front stretched for more than 750 km. They were usually about 2 metres deep, dug into the thick mud, with sandbags and wooden planks to hold them up and barbed wire on the top to keep the enemy from entering. There were special areas known as dugouts for sleeping.

PEACE AT CHRISTMAS

> The space between the opposing armies' trenches was called 'no man's land' and could be as little as a few metres wide in some places. Often enemy soldiers could hear each other and even shout to each other. No man's land was littered with barbed wire, ammunition boxes, empty machine gun cartridges, shattered helmets and other war debris.

Soldiers lived in the trenches for months. They were muddy, damp and stinky. They were also very unhygienic and skin infections were common. One infection, known as 'trench foot', was due to never being able to get properly dry and was so severe that sometimes the only way to get rid of it was by amputating a soldier's foot. If it was left untreated, it could lead to death.

NO END IN SIGHT

Every so often, one side would launch an offensive (attack) or attempt to enter their enemy's trenches by 'going over the top' of their own trench and crossing no man's land. This was highly dangerous, thanks to the powerful machine guns used by both sides, which could fire up to 400 bullets per minute. Few soldiers ever made it to the enemy's trenches.

By December 1914, most people realised that the First World War would not be a short war after all. About four million soldiers had died already and it was hard to see how anyone might actually win. Christmas in 1914 was pretty bleak for everyone, but especially for the soldiers fighting at the front, who were exhausted, freezing cold and worried that they might never get home to their families. Despite all this, a glimmer of Christmas spirit somehow managed to find a way to shine in the muddy trenches of the First World War.

> Back home, many people knitted scarves which were sent to the front to keep the soldiers warm.

FESTIVITIES AND FOOTBALL

It's hard to imagine a less Christmassy place than the cold, muddy Western Front in 1914, but it seems that the magic of Christmas is strong enough to brighten the very worst of times and the grimmest of places. They may not have been surrounded by their families, but the soldiers had formed special bonds with each other to help them get through the harsh realities of war. They had somehow found reasons to smile and to joke amidst the hardships and fighting, and on Christmas Eve carols could be heard being sung at various points (and in different languages) on both sides of the trenches. It was a moment of Christmas magic. No one had planned it, but in the sectors where the two lines of trenches were closest together, enemies started shouting to each other and agreed not to fire any guns the next day, 25 December. It would be the best present they could give each other – peace, even if it was just for a day.

Most soldiers kept their word and on Christmas Day, the guns of the Western Front were largely silent, and their deafening boom was replaced with singing and the joyful sounds of Christmas cheer. It was amazing. Some soldiers didn't agree with the truce, but others ventured into no man's land to chat to soldiers from the other side and exchange food and drink. They met people who were experiencing exactly the same things as them, who were missing Christmas with their families and just wanted the war to be over as soon as possible.

Then, someone produced a ball (who knows where they had even got it from!) and something truly surprising happened: hundreds of soldiers from both sides started to play FOOTBALL! It wasn't an organised game, there were no teams and no one really kept score (some soldiers reported that the Germans had won 3–2 but it must have been hard to tell in all that mud, especially without VAR). Really,

PEACE AT CHRISTMAS

it was more of a huge kick-about, like the ones they used to have with their friends at the park when they were kids. It must have been the most fun the soldiers had had in months.

Sadly, the truce didn't last and the soldiers were soon ordered to go back to bombarding each other. However, many soldiers wrote to their families and told them about what had happened in the trenches on Christmas 1914.

Soon, stories about the truce were printed in British newspapers. Public opinions were divided about whether it was a wonderful moment or an unnecessary distraction from the war, but more than 100 years later, the story of the Western Front on 25 December 1914 still shows the incredible power of Christmas to bring people together.

Unfortunately, there were no further Christmas truces during the First World War and fighting went on for nearly four more years. Trench warfare continued, with both sides using poisonous gases from 1915 to try and gain an advantage. There were huge numbers of casualties – one million in the 1916 Battle of the Somme alone. The First World War ended in November 1918 when Germany's emperor gave up the throne because he realised that he could not win the war, and the new government surrendered.

The First World War ended at 11 a.m. on 11 November (the eleventh month) 1918. This date and time is still marked in many places across the world to remember those who died, from all sides.

STOCKING FILLER FACTS

A PLACE CALLED CHRISTMAS

We all know that Christmas can inspire peace, but did you know that Christmas has inspired place names, too? In fact, there are quite a few locations around the world named after it.

CHRISTMAS ISLAND

On 25 December 1643, Captain William Mynors of the East India Company saw an uninhabited island in the Indian Ocean. He was one of the first Europeans to spot it, and as far as anyone knows, no one in the area had seen it or given it a name. So he decided to name it Christmas Island in honour of the day he'd found it. Over the years people have come to live on the island, which now has a population of around 1,700 and is governed by Australia.

However, the most famous residents are actually... red crabs, and there are more than 100 MILLION of them on Christmas Island! The crabs usually live in the forest but come to the ocean to breed. Breeding season on Christmas Island is a spectacular sight as the entire crab population swarms towards the sea between October and January.

NATAL, BRAZIL

Indigenous people have lived on the east coast of South America for thousands of years. In the sixteenth century, the Portuguese began to colonise the area – taking it over by force.

PEACE AT CHRISTMAS

One of the cities they founded was given a new name on Christmas Day 1597 by the Portuguese people who had taken over the country. Natal means Christmas in Portuguese, and they continued the Christmas theme by naming the nearby fort built to keep control of the city *Três Reis Magos* (the Three Kings).

Colonisation had an extremely negative impact on the populations that already lived in what became known as Brazil, and its effects are still being felt to this day.

CHRISTMAS, MICHIGAN, USA

This small town in the USA got its name from a factory that was built nearby to manufacture Christmas items. Nowadays, the town embraces its name by celebrating Christmas all year round with giant statues of Santa and Christmas-themed names everywhere.

CHAPTER 4

THE MOONS OF CHRISTMAS

On 25 December 1968, the crew of the Apollo 8 spacecraft became the first people to spend Christmas Day in space. Astronauts Frank Borman, Jim Lovell and Bill Anders were on a six-day mission to become the first humans to orbit the Moon.

At that time, it was the furthest that humans had ever travelled in space, and this mission paved the way for people to land on the Moon less than a year later. As Christmases go, it was a pretty quiet one up there in space, but also a historic one that had taken years of planning. And the crew found a very traditional way to celebrate up there on the big day . . .

RACE TO THE MOON

In the 1950s and 1960s, the USA and the Soviet Union (an empire ruled by Russia) were locked in a 'Space Race' to see who could explore the universe first. At the beginning, the Soviet Union seemed to have the edge, launching the first satellite, the first man and the first woman into space. By the 1960s, the most important goal of the Space Race was to land humans on the Moon, and this time the USA was determined to be first.

So, in 1961, US President John F. Kennedy announced that the USA would land a human on the Moon by the end of that decade – even though the total time spent in space by US astronauts up to that point was just fifteen minutes. President Kennedy's declaration was bold, and it meant that NASA had a lot of work to do to make it happen. First, they focused on the Mercury program from 1961 to 1963, which developed and tested one-person space missions. When this proved successful, they moved on to the Gemini program and a series of two-person missions. By 1966, NASA had successfully managed to send a crew into space for two weeks. But they weren't quite ready to reach the Moon yet.

THE APOLLO PROGRAMME

If the USA wanted to land astronauts on the Moon, they not only had to make sure that they had the power and technology to get them there, but they also needed to be able to get them back to Earth safely. The next step in their mission to the Moon was the Apollo program. NASA needed to make sure that the huge Saturn V rocket and the Apollo spacecraft needed to launch and carry astronauts to the Moon, were safe, so they tested them thoroughly, as well as other smaller rockets. After five successful uncrewed Apollo missions, NASA was ready to send humans into space again. On 11 October 1968, the Apollo 7 mission blasted off with a three-person crew and they successfully orbited the Earth 163 times, spending nearly eleven days in space.

> The Apollo 7 crew had a video camera on board and were able to hold video press conferences as well as record what they saw in space.

GOING FOR IT

Although the US space programme was progressing well by December 1968, they hadn't even reached the Moon, let alone landed on it. Time was running out to keep President Kennedy's word. So NASA decided to take things a BIG step forward with their next mission, Apollo 8.

THE MOONS OF CHRISTMAS

They would use the Saturn V rocket to launch an Apollo spacecraft to the Moon with a human crew. They were confident that they had the technology, the experience and the astronauts to succeed.

> The Saturn V rocket was 111 metres tall – that's as big as a 36-storey building – and weighed about as much as 400 elephants.

There was no time to waste, so on 21 December 1968, Frank Borman, Jim Lovell and Bill Anders said farewell and Merry Christmas to their loved ones and blasted off into space, hoping to be back in time for New Year.

It took nearly three days, but on 24 December, Apollo 8 reached the Moon and began to orbit it. The crew became the first-ever people to see the far side of the Moon and send back live videos of the Moon's surface. They took lots of photos and recorded valuable information for subsequent Apollo missions.

> Bill Anders also took the first colour photograph of Earth from space. Known as 'Earthrise', it showed our planet appearing above the Moon and has become an iconic image.

FIRST CHRISTMAS IN SPACE

They were very busy taking amazing pictures and collecting important data, but the Apollo 8 crew didn't forget it was Christmas. Although they missed their families, on 25 December they were able to eat the first-ever 'Christmas dinner' in space, complete with turkey, gravy and cranberry sauce. Not only was it a welcome Christmas treat to remind them of home, but it also marked a major improvement in space food in general. It was the first time that 'wet' food had been eaten in space – before this, astronauts had to add water to dry food, then squeeze it to mix it all up and eat it through a special feeder, which was not very appetising. This Christmas dinner tasted good, smelled great and could be eaten with a spoon!

THE MOONS OF CHRISTMAS

Apollo 8 returned safely to Earth on 27 December, so hopefully the crew's family had saved them some turkey and Santa had left them some presents. Then, on 20 July 1969, Neil Armstrong became the first person to walk on the Moon. It meant that NASA did manage to fulfil President Kennedy's promise and land on the Moon before the end of the 1960s, and before anyone else.

GOING FURTHER

Amazingly, not long after successfully landing on the Moon, humans stopped sending missions there. The main reason was that it was just too expensive. The Apollo programme, for example, cost nearly $26 billion, which would be more like $257 billion today. Fortunately, humans didn't stop venturing into space altogether – they just changed their approach and built space stations instead so that astronauts could spend longer periods away from Earth.

Space exploration also became more concerned with places that were much further away than the Moon too (the Moon is only 384,400 km from Earth, after all). These missions were too far for humans to travel, so some clever people had to think of new ways to find out what's out there. And once again, Christmas was the perfect time to do it.

THE MOONS OF CHRISTMAS

A LESS SUCCESSFUL CHRISTMAS

On 25 December 2003, ESA's (the European Space Agency's) *Mars Express* spacecraft entered orbit around Mars and attempted to make contact with its lander, *Beagle 2*, which had been released six days earlier (a lander is a spacecraft designed to land on a surface in space). Unfortunately, Beagle 2 failed to respond and eventually was given up as lost.

Despite this Christmas mishap, the Mars Express mission was still a success as even from its orbit above the planet, it was able to scan the surface and study what was happening there. In fact, the *Mars Express* is still in operation today and has been sending images and data back to Earth for more than twenty years.

> *Beagle 2* was actually spotted on the surface of Mars in 2015 in images sent back from a NASA orbiter. It had landed safely but failed to transmit.

CHRISTMAS ON ANOTHER MOON

Exactly a year later, on 25 December 2004, ESA were hoping for a more successful Christmas Day in space than the previous one. This time, they were hoping to launch a probe that would be able to explore Saturn's largest moon, Titan.

In a joint mission, NASA's Cassini orbiter carried ESA's Huygens probe on a 1.25 billion km, seven-year journey (which probably felt about as long as a Christmas game of Monopoly with your family). The Huygens probe was aiming to be the first human-made object to discover the secrets of Titan, which scientists believed might be similar to how Earth was 3.8 billion years ago, just before life began.

> Gian Domenico Cassini was a French astronomer who discovered four of Saturn's 274 moons and a large gap in Saturn's rings (which was named after him), and Dutch scientist Christiaan Huygens first discovered Saturn's rings and Titan.

THE MOONS OF CHRISTMAS

CHRISTMAS FLY-BY

This time the Christmas spirit was strong in space, and on Earth too! The mission control teams on Earth wore Santa hats and ate festive-themed snacks to send the probe off in style. Although the festive launch went well (and sounded like a lot of fun), it took twenty days for the probe to reach Titan's surface. The Christmas decorations would have been put away and New Year's resolutions made and broken by the time it landed on 14 January 2005!

However, during its journey, the probe had been busy investigating Titan's atmosphere – its chemistry, weather, temperature, and more. When it did finally land, the probe's mission was complete, as it had not been designed to survive the landing.

The Cassini, however, remained in orbit for another thirteen years, circling Saturn nearly 300 times and collecting amazing data. It took a closer look at Saturn's rings, found SEVEN new moons and mapped many others, as well as discovering more than ever before about their size, geography and chemistry.

Cassini performed more than 100 'flybys' of Titan, discovering hydrocarbon rivers, lakes, seas and even an ocean beneath its surface.

Twenty years after it left Earth, the Cassini mission ended (as planned). On 15 September 2017, with fuel running out, the orbiter plunged towards Saturn's surface and inevitable destruction.

STOCKING FILLER FACTS

CHRISTMAS DAY IN SPACE

The Apollo 8 crew might have been the first people to spend Christmas in space in 1968, but they were definitely not the last.

CHRISTMAS DAY 1973

In 1973, NASA built its first space station, Skylab, so that crews could observe space for longer periods. On Christmas Day, three astronauts were stationed there. After a seven-hour spacewalk, they returned to Skylab to eat Christmas dinner, including fruit cake for dessert, before opening presents and calling their families via satellite. They even built a Christmas tree out of leftover food tins.

CHRISTMAS DAY FIRSTS

On Christmas Day 1994, Russian astronaut Yelena Kondakova became the first woman to spend Christmas in space. In 1995, German astronaut Thomas Reiter became the first person who wasn't from Russia or the USA to spend Christmas Day in space.

CHRISTMAS DAY 2000

The ISS (International Space Station) is a spacecraft and science lab that is in permanent orbit above the Earth. The first piece of the ISS was launched in 1998 and it was completed in 2011. By 2000, though, the ISS was ready for people to stay and on 25 December 2000, two Russians and one American astronaut spent the first Christmas aboard. They ate rehydrated turkey. Yum. Some presents were also delivered via space supply ship!

CHRISTMAS DAY 2010

The crew of the ISS awoke to find Christmas stockings from their families hanging on the doors of their sleeping compartments. Who knew Santa delivered to space...!

CHRISTMAS DAY 2012

Canadian astronaut Chris Hadfield brought his guitar to the ISS and serenaded his crew with some Christmas songs in 2012.

CHRISTMAS DAY 2019

Nowadays technology means that the ISS even has Wi-Fi, but things can still go wrong... On Christmas Day 2019, British astronaut Tim Peake was trying to call his family when he dialled the wrong number and spoke to a complete stranger instead. She dismissed it as a festive prank when he said, 'Hello, is this planet Earth?'!

CHAPTER 5

SUPER SPORTY CHRISTMAS

On 25 December 1965 a crowd of 21,000 people watched Blackpool beat Blackburn Rovers 4–2 in the last ever league match to be played on Christmas Day in England. However, this definitely wasn't the end of festive football in the UK – it just meant that for ONE day at least, something was officially considered more important than football.

THE SECRET HISTORY OF CHRISTMAS

FOOTBALL AT CHRISTMAS

Christmas games have long been an important part of the UK football calendar, for a very good reason. In the past, most people had very few days off work during the year, but Christmas Day was a public holiday. Having games on Christmas Day meant that more people would be able to go and watch (in person, not on TV – this was back before they were invented!). When 26 December (aka Boxing Day) also became a public holiday in 1871, matches would be held then too – meaning that often teams played two games in two days!

However, as things changed, people began to get more time off over Christmas and they wanted to spend 25 December at home with their families. Gradually, the popularity of Christmas Day football matches went down. With fewer people going to work, public transport services were also greatly reduced on Christmas Day so it became more difficult to travel to matches. Also, with the widespread introduction of floodlights in the 1950s, games could be played in the evenings, after most people had finished work. There just wasn't such a need to cram quite soooo many fixtures into the festive period.

> The last Christmas Day matches in Scotland were played in 1976. Clydebank and St Mirren drew 2–2 and Alloa beat Cowdenbeath 2–1.

A FESTIVE BREAK?

You might think that with no games on Christmas Day, footballers would be able to relax over Christmas, just like we do. Unfortunately not, at least in the UK. In many countries where Christmas is widely celebrated, there are no football matches during the festive period, with some players getting up to two weeks off. However, in the UK there's no way that anyone could go without football for that long, so there's a full programme of fixtures on Boxing Day. Phew!

This actually means that footballers in the UK don't really get a Christmas break at all, because while we're busy opening our presents and stuffing our faces, they have to train on Christmas Day to prepare for a match the next day. They have to leave their families and friends to enjoy the festivities while they go and run around on a (probably) freezing cold pitch. But at least they might not have to do the washing up . . .

> Women were not encouraged to play football for many years – in fact females were banned from playing on official pitches in from 1921 to 1970. Despite this, some women's team flourished, including the pioneering Dick, Kerr Ladies, who played their first-ever match on Christmas Day 1917.

CHRISTMAS WINNERS

Many incredible sporting achievements have taken place at Christmas over the years. For these special people, Christmas is about winning! (And we don't mean beating their parents at Monopoly.) From basketball to American football, cricket to darts, some of the most amazing sporting achievements have happened over Christmas.

A GOLDEN CHRISTMAS

On 25 December 1973, Dutch footballer Johan Cruyff got something way better than socks for Christmas when he won the Ballon d'Or (which means golden ball in French). This honour is awarded to the player voted the best in the world (until 2007 it was just awarded to players in Europe, though) and it was Cruyff's second trophy. He was admired for his dazzling skills and creative play, helping to bring glory to Ajax in his native Netherlands and Barcelona in Spain. He was also part of the Netherlands national team that pioneered 'total football', an attacking style of play where everyone except the goalie swaps positions throughout the game, depending on what is happening in the match. It takes a lot of skill, awareness and clever play to do this, and Cruyff was one of the best at it.

Cruyff won his third Ballon d'Or in 1974 and his trademark turn, named after him, is still used today. He would pretend to pass in one direction but instead quickly drag the ball behind him before turning 180 degrees and dribbling away in another direction, leaving the opposition confused and standing in the wrong spot. Genius.

A CHRISTMAS COMEBACK

In the USA, Christmas Day games are played in sports such as basketball and football (the American kind!). On 25 December 2016, an NBA (National Basketball Association) match between San Francisco's Golden State Warriors and the Cleveland Cavaliers saw one of the greatest sporting comebacks in history. With around nine minutes left on the clock, the Cavaliers overturned the Warriors' 14-point lead to win the game in the last three seconds. It would have been an amazing story on any day of the year, but it was EXTRA special because it happened on Christmas Day.

THE CAVALIERS' CHRISTMAS MIRACLE

Before their famous Christmas Day showdown, the Cavaliers and the Warriors had already battled it out over seven games in the NBA Finals earlier in the year. The Cavaliers had trailed 3–1 after four games but won three games in a row to take the series 4–3 and lift the NBA Finals trophy. The Warriors, with star players such as the fan-favourite Stephen Curry and high-scoring Kevin Durant (who had signed for them after the Finals), were hoping for some festive revenge in their Christmas Day rematch.

Things started off well for the Warriors, with Durant opening the scoring and getting 10 points in the first quarter. But every time the Warriors started to edge in front, the Cavaliers, led by the LEGENDARY LeBron James, came right back to keep the score pretty close, and at the halfway point, the Warriors were only narrowly in the lead, 55–52.

> LeBron James is the NBA's all-time leading point scorer, with more than 42,000 points in his amazing career. He is also the first NBA player to become a billionaire (while still a player).

SUPER SPORTY CHRISTMAS

The match continued in much the same way in the third quarter. But early in the fourth quarter, the Warriors started to build a sizable lead, and with nine minutes and thirty-four seconds left in the match, they were winning 94–80.

However, as we know, the Cavaliers were good at coming back when all seemed lost. So they certainly weren't finished yet, and with just two minutes to go, they managed to level the score at 103–all. Finally, the Cavaliers took the lead thanks to a lucky rebound, but the Warriors fought back to level the score before Steph Curry (of course) hit a three-pointer. With just over one minute left on the clock, the Warriors were in front again.

With time running out, the Cavaliers took a twenty-second timeout (each team is allowed seven timeouts in the game) and came out believing they could win. They managed to cut the Warriors' lead to just 1 point and then, with 3.4 seconds left of the game, Kyrie Irving scored a two-pointer. Game over? No way, not in basketball and certainly not at Christmas! There was still time for another timeout and for Kevin Durant (the top scorer in the whole match) to MISS a three-pointer. The Cavaliers had won the game by a SINGLE POINT, 109–108.

What a way to spend Christmas Day! Just watching it must have been exhausting, let alone playing in the epic match. While it was an amazing Christmas present for the Cleveland Cavaliers, the Golden State Warriors would have felt more disappointed than a kid who thought that Santa had forgotten to visit. Hopefully a belated Christmas dinner with their families cheered them up. And in 2017, the Warriors finally got their revenge on the Cavaliers by beating them 4–1 in the NBA Finals, with Kevin Durant voted the MVP (most valuable player).

> The NBA's Christmas Day matches are the most popular games of the season, with millions of people tuning in each year from more than 200 territories.

SUPER SPORTY CHRISTMAS

NFL RULES!

On 25 December 1971, the longest-ever NFL game was played (NFL stands for National Football League, which is a league for what people in the US call 'football' and what people outside the US call 'American football'.) In a Christmas Day clash, the Miami Dolphins beat the Kansas City Chiefs, but only after two periods of overtime.

This was actually the first time that NFL games had been televised at Christmas. NFL is the most popular sports league in the USA, with games regularly watched by more than 20 million people, so televising it was the obvious choice. Unfortunately what happened in that Christmas Day game in 1971 meant that it would be nearly twenty years before another NFL game was shown at Christmas.

IS IT DINNER TIME YET?

Most NFL games last for sixty minutes, but Miami Dolphins versus Kansas City Chiefs lasted for an incredible eighty-two minutes and forty seconds. With the scores level at 24–24 after sixty minutes, the match went into a period of overtime. When no one had scored after fifteen minutes, it went into a second period of overtime in which whoever scored first would win. Eventually, Miami Dolphins kicker Garo Yepremian scored a field goal (he kicked the ball about 34 metres through the Chiefs' goalposts) and ended the game. Yepremian was a hero and the Dolphins and their fans were overjoyed, but many viewers at home were not happy at all (and not just the Chiefs fans). Apparently lots of people complained that the super-long game meant that their Christmas dinner was late, or worse, completely ruined! So for a long time there was no NFL on Christmas Day after that. (Apparently Christmas dinner was more important!)

SUPER SPORTY CHRISTMAS

WHICH OTHER SPORTS ARE PLAYED AT CHRISTMAS?

Other sports are important parts of the festive calendar too, including cricket. Every year, a Boxing Day Test match is played in Melbourne, Australia, between the Australian national team and a visiting national team. It can last for up to five days (cricket matches are looooooooong). Every four years or so, the Boxing Day Test match is Australia versus England as part of the Ashes competition. This is a series of matches between England and Australia held roughly every two years and first played in 1877, in which the two teams compete for a tiny trophy filled with the ashes of a part of a cricket stump. (It sounds a bit odd, but it's really important to both sides to win it.) In 2010, one of the most exciting Boxing Day Ashes Tests ever (at least from an England point of view) saw England bowl the mighty Australia out for just 98 runs in the first innings and score 513 runs in their own innings. Australia scored 258 runs in their second innings, meaning that England won by 157 runs without even having to bat again. It also meant that England retained the Ashes trophy for the first time in nearly twenty-five years.

LET'S PLAY... DARTS!

Another sport that often crowns a festive champion is darts. The World Darts Championships takes place in the UK from mid-December to early January, which means that competitors from all over the world spend the festive period preparing for matches rather than going to Christmas parties, wrapping presents or relaxing with their families. In the 2023–24 tournament, sixteen-year-old Luke Littler from the UK finished in second place. (It was the first time he'd even entered!) But he did even better the year after, winning the tournament at the age of seventeen.

> Luke Littler is the youngest-ever darts world champion and he earned about £500,000 in prize money, which must have helped him buy some amazing belated Christmas presents for his family!

STOCKING FILLER FACTS

CHRISTMAS TRADITIONS

There are some amazing traditions from all over the world that people in different countries incorporate into the festive period, and they don't all involve sport!

CHRISTMAS TREES

Many families decorate real or artificial trees in their homes at Christmas and put their presents underneath them. People all around the world have been doing this for centuries, but the tradition only started in the UK when Queen Victoria and her family made it popular in the mid-nineteenth century. Fir trees are popular choices, but New Zealanders prefer the *pōhutukawa* (pronounced poh-hoo-tuh-kah-wuh). It bursts into festive red flowers in December.

DENMARK

Before opening presents, it's traditional in many Danish homes to dance around the Christmas tree, holding hands with your family while singing Christmas songs.

AVOIDING THE COLD IN ICELAND

Jólabókaflóð (pronounced yo-la-bok-a-flot), the Christmas book flood, happens on Christmas Eve in Iceland. People exchange gifts of books and then snuggle up in front of the fire and start reading them straight away.

CHRISTMAS FIREWORKS

Some central American countries, such as El Salvador, like to start Christmas Day with a bang. Fireworks displays are popular on 24 and 25 December.

A WHEELY-FUN ONE

In Caracas, Venezuela, it has become traditional for many people to roller-skate to Midnight Mass on Christmas Eve. No one knows why or when this started, but these days the roads are even closed to make it safer.

A CHRISTMAS... SPIDER?

Christmas decorations are usually bright and sparkly and not at all subtle. You may expect to see a robin perched on a snowy Christmas branch or a reindeer plodding through some snow. However, in Ukraine most people have at least one spider's web decoration on their tree. It honours a legend in which a poor woman had no money for decorations so a spider covered her tree in a glittering web.

CHAPTER 6

CHRISTMAS DAY HEIST

On 25 December 1950, four people took a very important slab of rock from Westminster Abbey in England and transported it to Scotland. As heists go it was a pretty daring one. But it wasn't carried out because of greed or even mischief, but instead because the people who took it believed they were doing the right thing.

The Stone of Scone,* also known as the Stone of Destiny, was a legendary piece of stone that had been an important part of coronation ceremonies in Scotland since the Middle Ages. So, how did it end up in England, why did four people give up their Christmas Day (one of the BEST days of the year) to steal it and where is the Stone of Scone now?

LEGENDARY ROCK

No one knows exactly where the Stone of Scone came from. Some legends say it was used as a pillow by Jacob, an important person in the Bible (that must have been uncomfortable!). Other stories say it came from Ireland, while others claim it was taken from the Antonine Wall, built by the Romans in Scotland. Geologists in the twentieth century concluded that the stone was almost certainly from Scotland. But wherever it came from, this stone was IMPORTANT, and from the ninth century Scottish kings and queens would sit on it when they were crowned.

---

*Usually pronounced 'skoon', but some people say 'skon' and others 'skown'.

These coronations took place at Scone Palace, Perthshire, so the rock became known as the Stone of Scone.

Another legend said that the stone was associated with Fergus Mór mac Eirc, the ruler of an ancient kingdom that stretched from western Scotland across to north-eastern Ireland.

STOLEN!

The stone was first stolen nearly 700 years ago, long before the Christmas Day heist took place. In 1296, the English King Edward I (not the Edward mentioned in chapter 1) took the stone while he was trying to invade Scotland. Of course, Edward probably didn't march into Scone Palace himself and heave it out with his own royal hands – he most likely had some strong soldiers do it for him and then carry it all the way back to England.

Edward I was determined to conquer Scotland and hoped that possessing the Stone of Scone would give him authority there. (It didn't, it just made Scottish people like him even less.) He was nicknamed 'the Hammer of the Scots' because he tried to invade several times and make Scottish people accept his rule. Edward did win a few battles, but he was famously halted by Scottish forces led by the legendary William Wallace and Robert the Bruce. In 1307, Edward marched his army to the border between England and Scotland in preparation for another invasion, but he died before he could launch an attack.

> Edward was also nicknamed 'Longshanks' because he was apparently very tall.

Before he died, Edward ordered an elaborate wooden Coronation Chair to be built, decorated with golden animals and plants, with the Stone of Scone hidden underneath the seat. It was placed in Westminster Abbey, and the chair has been used in nearly forty coronations since then.

'WE WANT IT BACK!'

In 1603, England and Scotland were united when they had the same king, James I (in Scotland he was actually James VI), who succeeded his cousin Elizabeth I. It meant that the Stone of Scone was once again being used to crown Scottish monarchs.

However, many Scottish people (and lots of English people too) felt that the stone belonged back in Scotland. Over the centuries, various Scottish leaders asked for it back – there was even a bill (proposal for a new law) about it in the House of Commons in 1924. Even still, the Stone of Scone was not returned and it became an important symbol for the Scottish nationalist movement (a group of people who felt that Scotland should be a separate country with its own laws and government).

> In 1914, a small bomb was placed near the Coronation Chair, allegedly by the suffragettes (who were campaigning for women's right to vote). Although the chair was damaged slightly when it exploded, the Stone of Scone was fine.

By Christmas 1950, the Stone of Scone had been in England for so long that it seemed like it would never be returned to Scotland. But a group of students from Glasgow, Scotland, decided to take matters into their own hands while they had some free time during the Christmas holidays. Law student Ian Hamilton, along with Kay Matheson, Gavin Vernon and Alan Stuart were all supporters of Scottish nationalism and were keen to take action to restore what they saw as Scotland's symbol. They hatched a plan so daring that it seemed unlikely that they would succeed, but incredibly, they did.

THE HEIST

On 23 December, while their families and friends were safe and cosy at home, the students, in two separate cars, drove hundreds of miles along snow-covered roads from Glasgow to London. They made it, and on Christmas Eve they put their plan into action. As the Abbey closed for the night, Ian hid in a dark corner and waited for everyone to leave so he could steal the Stone of Scone. However, a security guard saw him and escorted him out, believing Ian's story that he'd been locked in 'by accident'. (He must have been a good actor, eh?)

The students came up with a Plan B, and very early on Christmas Day 1950, they put it into action. At 4 a.m. they parked close to the Abbey, and while Kay kept watch outside, the other three broke into the building. It was pitch-black inside, and with only a small torch to guide their way, they headed for the Coronation Chair as quickly as they could. Clumsily, the group pulled the stone from its place under the Chair. It was much heavier than they'd imagined and the three students DROPPED IT ON THE

FLOOR, breaking the famous Stone of Scone into two pieces. That was definitely not part of the plan.

A shocked Ian picked up the smaller piece and ran out of the Abbey with it. He just had time to throw it into the back of his car and put his coat over it before a passing police officer stopped to ask him what he was doing. It was certainly a bit late to be hanging around Westminster Abbey, especially on Christmas Day, but a quick-thinking Ian just said that he and Kay were looking for a hotel and then pretended to drive away. So, when Gavin and Alan came running out of the Abbey, they thought that Ian and Kay had left them behind. Worse still, Ian had the keys to the second car, so they had to escape on foot!

In fact, Ian had dropped those car keys in the Abbey, so he went back to retrieve them – and the other part of the Scone of Scone. While Kay drove the first piece of the Stone to Birmingham, to hide it in her friend's garage, Ian managed to get the large piece into the boot of his car, single-handedly.

BACK TO SCOTLAND

As Ian drove away, he saw Gavin and Alan walking along the road. Together they concocted a plan to bury half of the Stone of Scone in a field somewhere in Kent, England.

It wasn't long before people realised that the Stone of Scone was missing. The Police thought that the Stone would be heading to Scotland, so they closed the England/Scotland border (for the first time in 400 years) and searched every car heading that way. They also searched ports and airfields, just to be on the safe side. But of course, as they weren't searching garages in Birmingham or fields in Kent, they didn't find it.

On New Year's Eve 1950, Ian, Gavin and Alan went back to the field in Kent to dig up the largest part of the stone, but they found some people camping right on top of it! They managed to retrieve it and drove it back to Scotland where they handed it over to some friends, who put it under the floorboards of a factory for safekeeping. When the other piece arrived from Birmingham, a stone mason put the halves back together again.

THE STONE OF SCONE IS REVEALED

For three months, police officers searched the whole country, but they didn't find any trace of the Stone of Scone. It meant, though, that the group who had stolen it were faced with a dilemma: they didn't want to keep the important national symbol hidden, but if they revealed it, they would probably get into trouble. In the end, they decided to leave the stone where people would find it. So they placed it, draped in the Scottish flag, in the ruins of Arbroath Abbey, which was a place of great significance to Scottish nationalists.

> In 1320, the Declaration of Arbroath was a famous letter written by the nobles of Scotland to the Pope (head of the Catholic Church) asking him to recognise Scotland's independence from England.

The Police soon worked out who had been responsible for taking the Stone, but no one got into trouble. (The UK government didn't want to stir up support for Scottish nationalism by putting the four students in prison.) Instead, the Stone was returned to Westminster Abbey on 11 April 1951 and put back into the Coronation Chair. It was used two years later for the Coronation of Queen Elizabeth II.

RETURNED TO SCOTLAND

Although the students who took the Stone on Christmas Day 1950 did not succeed in keeping it in Scotland at that time, it was eventually returned to Scotland, officially and permanently, in 1996, by Queen Elizabeth II and the UK Prime Minister. All four of the people involved lived to see this moment, forty-six years after carrying out the theft.

At first, the Stone of Scone was kept on display in Edinburgh Castle. Nowadays, it can be seen at the Perth Museum in Scotland, although it was removed temporarily and taken back to Westminster Abbey for the coronation of King Charles III in May 2023.

The leader of the student robbers, Ian Hamilton, went on to become a very well-respected lawyer and was awarded the status of KC (King's Counsel) for his professional excellence, so we can be pretty sure that after 1950, the only Christmas Day 'heists' he committed were taking the last roast potato or stealing an extra mince pie!

CHRISTMAS DAY HEIST

STOCKING FILLER FACTS

MERRY CRIME-MAS

The robbery of the Stone of Scone happened on Christmas Day 1950, but there have been other Christmas crimes over the years. Here are some of the weirdest.

THE SANTA CLAUS BANK ROBBERY

At midday on 23 December 1927, 'Santa' visited a bank in Cisco, Tesco, USA a day and a half early and in broad daylight. In fact, this fake Santa was one of four men who were robbing the bank, and his sack was filled with stolen money, not presents.

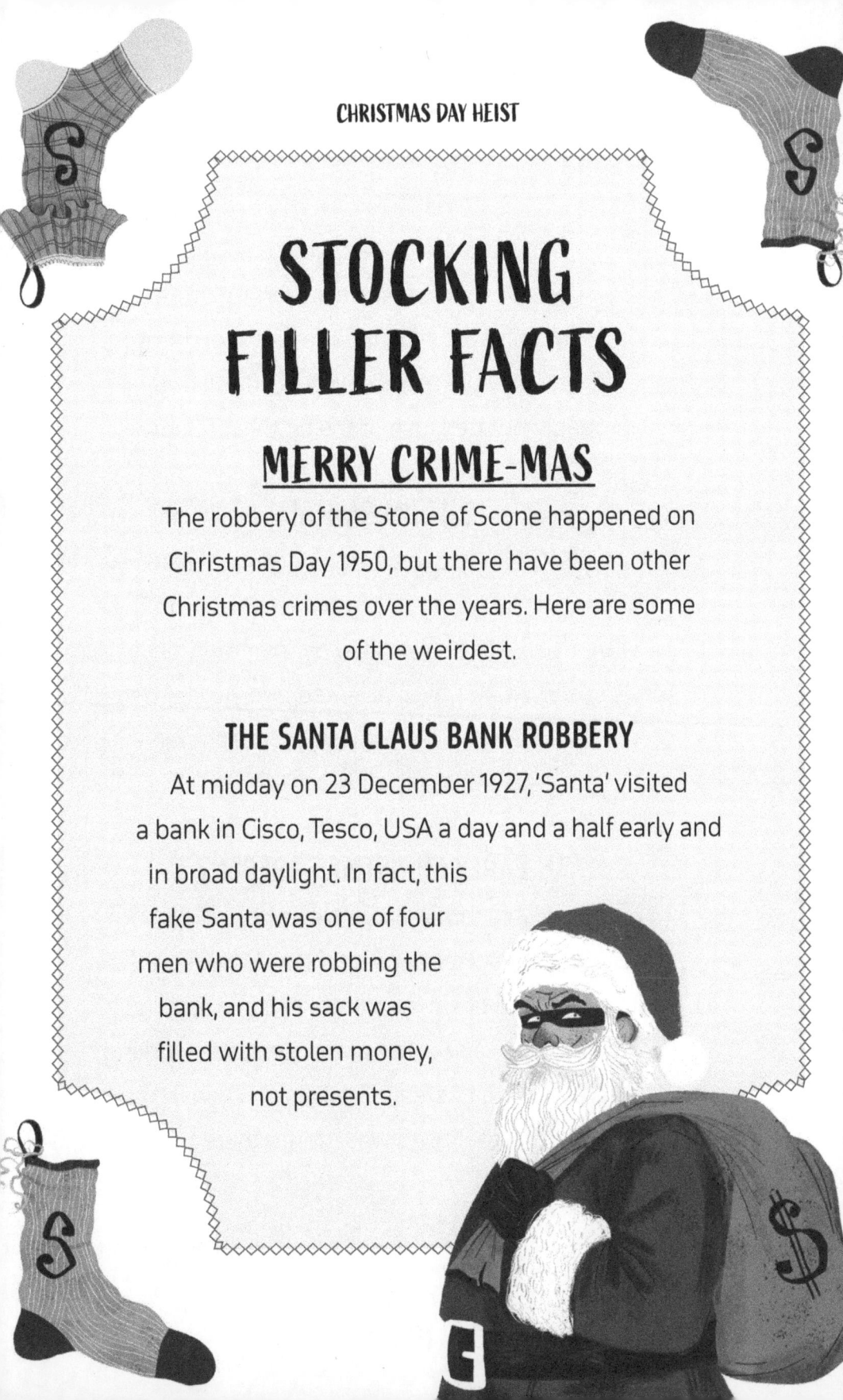

The robbers managed to escape, so the desperate police issued a picture of Santa and asked if anyone had seen him! Eventually the robbers were caught, but probably not because of the picture of Santa.

BUT I'M SANTA!

In 2010, a would-be burglar got stuck in a chimney while trying to break into a house in the USA. He had to be released by the emergency services and when police arrested him, he claimed to be Santa. They didn't believe him, of course – it was clearly a ho-ho-hoax!

AN EARLY CHRISTMAS PRESENT

This robbery occurred on 26 November 1983 from the Brinks-Mat warehouse near London's Heathrow Airport. A gang of six men entered the warehouse (with help from a security guard who was working there) hoping to steal £3 million in cash that they believed was stored there.

CHRISTMAS DAY HEIST

However, they actually found nearly 7,000 gold bars worth around £26 million. Christmas had come early for them! So they loaded the gold into their van, plus £100,000 in diamonds. As they left the warehouse, the gang cheerfully wished the terrified security guards a 'Merry Christmas'.

Although two members of the gang were caught and sent to prison, along with several people who helped them melt and sell the gold, the rest of the gang has never been caught and a large part of the Brinks-Mat gold is still unaccounted for.

CHAPTER 7

THE FIRST CHRISTMAS?

No one is sure exactly when people began celebrating Christmas, but 25 December 336 CE is the first one that appears on any official records. It's likely that it wasn't the first EVER, but it is important because we know for sure that it happened and how it was celebrated.

It took place during the time of the Roman Empire and it was all Emperor Constantine I's idea. The Roman Empire was huge and included parts of what is now Europe, northern Africa and western Asia. This means that the people we call 'Romans' were actually from lots of different countries, followed many religions and spoke many languages. Constantine was a Christian who came from what is now Serbia and wanted all Romans to celebrate his chosen religion.

A GOOD DAY TO CELEBRATE

When Constantine decided to pick a day to commemorate the birth of Jesus, he chose 25 December because it matched the dates of two other popular Roman winter festivals called Saturnalia and Dies Natalis Solis Invicti (the Birth of the Invincible Sun).

Saturnalia was in honour of Saturn, the Roman god of agriculture (farming), and Romans celebrated by eating special food, exchanging gifts and lighting candles. It was a public holiday that lasted several days, so it was not just 25 December. Instead of going to work, everyone relaxed and had fun. In fact, Saturnalia was mostly a massive days-long party, with everyone letting their hair down and celebrating together in the streets.

> During Saturnalia, enslaved people were given temporary freedom and often served food by their masters instead of having to serve them.

Special events were often held during Saturnalia in arenas known as amphitheatres. People would take fancy foods to eat while they watched performances such as contests between female gladiators. Some people would dress up as kings, to represent Saturn, and sweet pastries with fruit inside were a popular snack (a bit like mince pies are today).

The other popular Roman festival at this time, Dies Natalis Solis Invicti, was dedicated to the birthday of the sun god (Sol Invictus). It also involved giving presents, as well as making wishes and kissing each other under mistletoe, a plant that often grows on other trees.

Unlike Saturnalia, Dies Natalis Solis Invicti did fall on 25 December. It was a joyful time, with chariot races held in the sun god's honour and a feast at the end of the day. Sol Invictus was an important part of Roman culture, and Emperor Aurelian (who ruled from 270 to 275 CE) was a dedicated follower. He put an image of Sol Invictus on Roman coins, named them the god of soldiers and built a temple in their honour.

> During Dies Natalis Solis Invicti, people often decorated their houses with greenery, which also sounds quite Christmassy.

THE FIRST CHRISTMAS?

A VERY MERRY CHRISTMAS

Deciding to celebrate Christmas on 25 December was a very clever idea. Romans were already in the habit of celebrating at that time of year, so Christmas fitted right in. The more the merrier!

You might assume that the Romans, and Emperor Constantine in particular, were the ones who made Christmas what it is today, but it's really only part of the story. In fact, just like Saturnalia and Dies Natalis Solis Invicti, winter festivals have been a big part of human life since the first civilisations walked the Earth.

> We have the Romans to thank for lots of important inventions, including concrete and the calendar. They also helped to develop roads, sewers and the Latin alphabet.

CHRISTMAS'S ANCIENT RELATIVES

To understand the importance of ancient winter festivals, we need to try and imagine what life was like thousands of years ago. Nowadays we know a lot about how the world works, such as how the Earth changes over time, why weather happens, what shape our planet is and who lives on it. Although we still have a lot to learn, we know waaaaay more than people did thousands of years ago. They had no idea why it would rain on some days and not on others, why some things tasted delicious and other things made them sick, why the sea moved but the land stood still. They must have had so many questions!

Although clever people would have been able to explain some things by noticing patterns in nature, other things would have just been baffling. How do you explain rainbows, lightning or thunder, for example, without a lot of complicated science? People thought that there must be powerful forces at work, such as gods, which should be feared, praised or celebrated.

THE FIRST CHRISTMAS?

As the Romans thought, one of these powerful forces had an obvious influence: the Sun. People noticed that at certain times of the year days were longer and nights shorter, and at other times the days were shorter and nights were longer. They began to hold special celebrations to mark the two points in the year when the days were at the longest and shortest, known as the solstices.

WHY SOLSTICES HAPPEN

The Earth, which is tilted and constantly spinning, orbits the Sun. It takes Earth twenty-four hours (one day) to do a full rotation and 365.25 days (one year) to complete a single orbit of the Sun. Earth's two halves are known as the northern and southern hemispheres; they each have a pole at the far end and are divided by an imaginary line known as the equator. When one pole is closest to the Sun, days are longer and nights are shorter in that hemisphere (meaning it's summer) and the opposite is happening in the other hemisphere (meaning it's winter). A solstice occurs on the day when Earth's poles are at their most tilted towards or away from the Sun.

> Solstice comes from the Latin words meaning 'sun' and 'stand still'.

YULE LOVE THIS ONE

For many people, the winter solstice became their most important celebration, as it marked the mid-point of winter and they could celebrate that the days would become longer from then on. Winter can be dark and dreary, so finding a reason to celebrate and look forward to spring (especially in times when they didn't have electricity, heating or Netflix) would have been really important. The ancient monument Stonehenge in the UK has been used to celebrate the winter and summer solstices for thousands of years.

THE FIRST CHRISTMAS?

We've already learnt about Saturnalia and Dies Natalis Solis Invicti, but other areas developed different winter celebrations, traces of which can also be seen today in many Christmas traditions. The Vikings and other northern European people celebrated a twelve-day festival known as Jul (or Yule). They marked the solstice by bringing an entire tree trunk, or Yule log, into their homes and burning it to symbolise light in the darkness and to bring good luck. They also decorated trees and made wreaths, which are traditions that are also seen at Christmas.

Nowadays many people also enjoy a yule log at Christmas, but it's a log-shaped chocolate cake and they eat it rather than burn it!

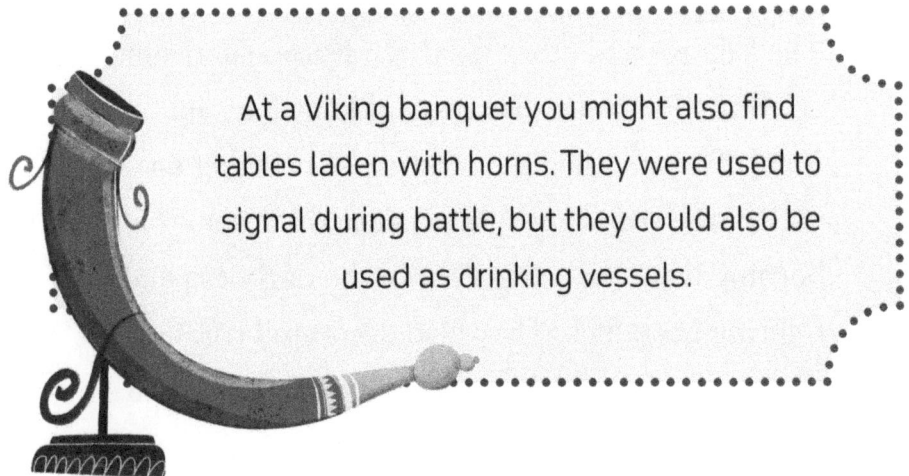

At a Viking banquet you might also find tables laden with horns. They were used to signal during battle, but they could also be used as drinking vessels.

FESTIVALS OF LIGHT

The idea of celebrating light during the darkness of winter can be seen in many festivals from around the world. Yalda or Shab-e Yalda is an ancient Persian festival that celebrates the birth of the sun god, Mithra, and the triumph of light over darkness. Nowadays many people in Iran and nearby countries such as Afghanistan and Azerbaijan eat nuts and pomegranates to celebrate, and some people even stay up all night to welcome the sunrise.

For the ancient Maya people who lived in what is now Mexico and other parts of central America, the sun was extremely important. They used it in their daily life to tell the time and also believed that the sun god was one of several nature gods watching over them. The winter solstice was a very special time of year for the Maya. Although it was the darkest and longest day of the whole year, they celebrated it as the moment of the sun's rebirth. For the Maya, the winter solstice was a time of renewal and hope because it meant that spring was coming. It was a time to get together with family and look forward to the next year.

Hanukkah, the Jewish festival of light, also takes place around the time of the winter solstice (although the date each year is actually decided by a lunar calendar). Traditions at Hanukkah include lighting candles, exchanging gifts and money (gelt), playing games and eating special foods such as doughnuts and latkes.

The Indigenous Hopi people of what is now Arizona, USA, have celebrated Soyal around this time for thousands of years. The Soyal festival welcomes the sun back from its winter 'sleep' and involves blessings and lots of dancing.

SUMMER CHRISTMAS

Of course, it's only winter in the northern hemisphere on 25 December, so for anyone in the southern hemisphere who celebrates Christmas, it's a summer festival. In the southern hemisphere, the winter solstice is in June. So this is when the ancient Incas, who lived in parts of South America, held their winter festival Inti Raymi, to honour their sun god.

No one lives permanently in Antarctica, but scientists who live there during the winter celebrate Midwinter's Day (in June) by cutting a hole in the ice and taking a freezing dip in the Southern Ocean!

STOCKING FILLER FACTS

CHRISTMAS WEATHER

While some people hope for snow at Christmas, others love a sunny Christmas with trips to the beach.

COLD CHRISTMAS

The coldest place in December is usually Siberia in Russia, with an average temperature on Christmas Day of around -40°C, although it can go as low as -80°C.

HOT CHRISTMAS

One of the hottest places on Earth in December is usually Queensland in Australia, with temperatures of up to 51°C. It's definitely not the place to visit if you enjoy building snow people at Christmas.

A VERY WHITE CHRISTMAS

Many people dream of a snowy Christmas, but in 1974, parts of Czechia received more than 2 metres of snow at Christmas. That meant that most people who stepped outside would have been completely covered from head to toe in snow!

A GREEN CHRISTMAS

On Christmas Day 2022, a polar rain aurora that stretched for 3,000 km was visible across the North Pole. It produced a spooky green glow caused by charged particles flowing from the Sun, rather than the usual swirling pattern of the aurora borealis (Northern Lights).

AN ORANGE CHRISTMAS

A freak dust storm from the Sahara desert blocked out the sun on 22 December 2019, turning the skies orange in parts of Europe, including Italy.

CHAPTER 8

A CHRISTMAS VISITOR

On 25 December 1758, a German astronomer spotted something AMAZING in the night sky. It not only made his Christmas Day the best one ever, but also proved that an English man named Edmond Halley was really clever. It wasn't a sighting of Santa on his way back home to the North Pole for a well-deserved rest, though – it was a very special comet (no, NOT the famous reindeer called Comet!).

At that time, this comet did not have a name, but it soon got one: Halley's Comet, in honour of Edmond Halley, an astronomer who had predicted the exact year that it would appear. You might not think that knowing when a comet is going to appear is a very big deal. These days, we know when a lot of big astronomical events such as comets, eclipses and other extraordinary sights are going to happen. We're told when, where and how to see them, and then they happen, exactly as we were told they would. (Lucky us!)

However, back in 1758 no one had EVER correctly predicted when a comet would appear. But Edmond Halley believed that he had worked out how long this comet's orbit took (seventy-six years) and therefore when it would next appear. And on Christmas Day 1758, he was proved right.

Comets are a bit like giant space snowballs, except that they're made of dust, rock and gases, as well as ice. They orbit the Sun, but in a different way to planets like Earth. While Earth orbits pretty much in a circle, comets travel in a more oval-shaped path

A CHRISTMAS VISITOR

that can take them far out into the solar system and back again. A single orbit for a comet can last a few years, or even millions. When a comet gets close to the Sun, the intense heat makes them release gas and dust which eventually streams out like a long tail. Imagine how incredible they must look in the night sky!

> There are billions of comets in our solar systems and they're thought to be bits of debris left over from when the solar system was formed 4.6 billion years ago.

WORKING THINGS OUT

But how did Halley know when this comet would appear? Well the answer – and you might have been hoping for something a little more magical – is because he was really, really good at, drum roll please . . . MATHS!

Yep, maths. It turns out that maths is pretty important and people use it all the time. Edmond Halley was an astronomer, a scientist who studies the universe and everything in it, and a mathematician. Like most scientists, he was good at observing things (in his case, the universe), taking notes and then using that information to come up with theories about how things might work. One of the things he was keen to learn more about was comets, and in particular one that he had seen with his own eyes in 1682.

Scientists often work together or are inspired by other people's ideas, and Halley was lucky because he had a super-clever friend who had come up with some extraordinarily brilliant theories. His friend was called Isaac Newton (you've probably heard of him) and he was really into maths too. But he was also into physics, which is the study of matter, motion, forces and energy. Newton was interested in finding ways of explaining how and why the things in our universe behave in the way they do. It's pretty epic stuff, looking at everything from teeny-tiny atoms to enormous stars.

A CHRISTMAS VISITOR

Isaac Newton was born on Christmas Day 1642, so the comet named after his friend actually appeared on what would have been his 116th birthday!

When Halley mentioned to his friend Newton that he wanted to calculate different comets' orbits but wasn't too sure how things moved in space, Newton told him that he had the answers he needed. When Newton explained his groundbreaking ideas, Halley was so impressed that he thought the whole world needed to hear them. He encouraged Newton to publish his ideas in a book, so in 1687, he did, in a book called *Principia*.

> Many people believe that *Principia* is the foundation of modern science. It presented Newton's three laws of motion, which we still learn today, although later scientists such as Albert Einstein have developed further ideas too.

MAKING PREDICTIONS

Thanks to his friend Isaac Newton, Halley now had the information he needed to study comets in more detail. At that time, people really didn't know a huge amount about them. In ancient times, people had feared the sudden appearance of a blazing light in the sky, which could be visible for weeks or even months. They wondered what it could mean. Were they all doomed?

Even most scientists believed that comets just passed by once and were never seen again. However, inspired by Newton's ideas, Halley began to wonder if comets were actually following an orbit, just like

Earth, and that what we thought of as different comets were actually regular reappearances of the same comet.

Halley studied data on twenty-four different comets and used Newton's theories to predict their orbits. He found evidence to support his theory: comets had been sighted in 1531, 1607 and 1682 (he saw the last one himself) and he was convinced that they were the same one, with an orbit lasting between seventy-five and seventy-six years (orbits can vary slightly due to the effects of gravity from the different planets the comet passes). In 1705, Halley published his ideas and predicted that this comet would be seen again in 1758.

RIGHT ON TIME!

Unfortunately, Edmond Halley did not live to find out that he was absolutely right. He had been twenty-six when he saw the comet for the first time and would have been one hundred and two when it returned on Christmas Day 1758.

(He died at the pretty great age of eighty-five years old.) We're sure he would have been very proud to have had a comet named after him, though!

People soon realised that not only was Halley right about the comet's orbit, but that humans had actually seen it many times before over the centuries. It had been documented by Chinese astronomers as far back as 240 BCE; it's on the Bayeux Tapestry that shows the famous Battle of Hastings (see chapter 1); and it can be seen on a famous fourteenth-century Italian wall painting.

Halley's Comet was last seen on Earth in 1986, and because scientists knew it was coming, they were able to study it closely, even from space. Five spacecraft from different countries travelled together to meet the comet as it passed by Earth. They were able to take photos of it as well as analyse its size and what it is made of.

A CHRISTMAS VISITOR

We now know that Halley's Comet is about 15 km long and 8 km wide, and it is one of the darkest objects in the solar system. Its orbit is about 12.2 billion km.

The comet's orbit will be near Earth again in 2061, but no one knows yet whether it will be on Christmas Day. How old will you be when Halley's Comet next visits?

STOCKING FILLER FACTS

WORST CHRISTMAS EVER!

While Christmas 1758 was a brilliant one for the astronomer who spotted Halley's Comet, sometimes the big day doesn't always go as planned. From small setbacks to larger mishaps, let's take a look at some Christmas Days that weren't so great...

UN-MERRY CHRISTOPHER COLUMBUS

Christoper Columbus had famously 'discovered' America in 1492. (To be clear: he didn't, because lots of people were living there already, and anyway, he thought he was in Asia.) He was probably feeling pretty good about himself on his way back to Spain, until his ship, the *Santa María*, ran aground on a reef off Haiti on 25 December 1492.

A CHRISTMAS VISITOR

Columbus and the crew were fine, but the *Santa María* sank to the bottom of the sea and was lost forever.

(NO) CHRISTMAS DAY 1621

In the 1600s, many people moved from Europe to live in America and founded colonies. Many people brought their traditions and customs with them, while others wanted a fresh start. William Bradford, who was governor of the Plymouth Colony, decided that his community would be hardworking and religious. The only day off allowed would be Sundays. He objected strongly to games and doing things for enjoyment, so he also ruled that no one should celebrate Christmas. It was just too much fun!

(NO) CHRISTMAS DAY 1647

After the Civil War in Britain, King Charles I had been replaced by a government who wanted people to behave all the time.

They thought that Christmas encouraged people to party, so they weren't keen on it. In 1647, they banned Christmas celebrations altogether: no decorations, no carols, no presents and people had to go to work. A lot of people did not agree, so they had even bigger parties than usual in protest. However, the ban on Christmas lasted until 1660, when the monarchy was restored. Bah humbug!

CHRISTMAS DAY 1932

Thanks to the invention of the radio, in 1932, the British monarch was able to give their first-ever Christmas speech to the world. It was a big moment for King George V, and he probably felt a bit nervous, especially because it was being broadcast LIVE. Unfortunately, as he sat down to give his speech, seconds before going on air, the King's favourite chair collapsed underneath him. Luckily, he was unhurt – the same could not be said for the chair – and he carried on with the broadcast as if nothing had happened.

CHAPTER 9

A CHRISTMAS SURPRISE

On 25 December 1776, General George Washington led his troops across the freezing Delaware River from Pennsylvania to New Jersey in what is now the USA, hoping to give his enemies a very unwelcome Christmas surprise.

He wanted to catch them while they were feeling merry and a bit tired to gain a valuable advantage.

Washington's plan worked and set his side on a path to victory . . . er, eventually.

FIGHTING FOR INDEPENDENCE

Washington was fighting in the American Revolution, also known as the War of Independence. It began in 1775, but it had been simmering for far longer. People from Britain and other European countries had started to move to North America in the 1600s, building villages and towns on land that belonged to Native Americans, in an unjust process called colonisation. These new areas were then governed by the old countries that they had come from originally.

A few countries, such as France, Spain and the Netherlands, had colonies in America, but Great Britain had the most. By 1763, Britain had thirteen – Massachusetts, New Hampshire, Rhode Island, Connecticut, New York, Pennsylvania, Delaware, New Jersey, Maryland, Virginia, North Carolina, South Carolina and Georgia.

A CHRISTMAS SURPRISE

It must have seemed strange to be ruled by a country that was thousands of miles away. Britain passed many laws to make sure that the colonists paid lots of taxes, and if the colonists objected, the British just sent soldiers to enforce their laws.

> In 1773, the British government passed a law that British traders could sell tea at a better price than the colonists. In protest, the colonists boarded the British ships docked in Boston and threw all their tea into the sea. It became known as the Boston Tea Party.

After the Boston Tea Party, the British introduced even harsher laws. Although the colonists asked Britain to change them, they didn't and just sent even more soldiers. The colonists began to suspect that they wouldn't be able to find a peaceful solution to their situation and started to prepare for war.

WAR BREAKS OUT

The British did not want a war (they'd already fought quite a few in the sixteenth and seventeenth centuries) so in April 1775, they tried to destroy the colonists' supplies and make it impossible for them to fight. However, the colonists were warned they were coming and a group of minutemen (men ready to fight at a minute's notice) quickly intercepted the British at towns called Lexington and Concord, forcing them to turn back.

The Battles of Lexington and Concord marked the start of the American Revolution and were a major shock to the British. It showed that they could not underestimate the strength and determination of the colonists, and the colonists' success encouraged many others to join the fight. The next major battle, Bunker Hill, in June 1775, was also seen as a victory for the colonists. The British captured the Hill but lost so many soldiers in the process that many felt the other side were the real winners.

A CHRISTMAS SURPRISE

DECLARATION OF INDEPENDENCE

After that, both sides settled in for a long war, with the colonists laying siege to Boston (trapping the British there but not attacking them) and also heading for Quebec (in what is now Canada) to try to gather support from the people who lived there.

Although neither side could be said to be 'winning' at this point, the colonists were gathering more and more support, and on 4 July 1776, the thirteen colonies signed a joint Declaration of Independence from Great Britain, which officially created the United States of America. However, the British did not agree, so the war continued. In fact, by the summer of 1776, the British army was starting to take control, thanks to its larger size and better equipment. The colonists' Continental Army was pushed further and further west as the British advanced.

> 4 July is an important national holiday in the USA, when Americans join together to celebrate Independence Day with parades, fireworks, picnics and other special events.

By Christmas 1776, spirits in the Continental Army were low and many soldiers must have doubted that they would ever be truly independent. Christmas was looking pretty terrible, until General George Washington unwrapped his clever plan . . .

A CHRISTMAS VISIT

Crossing a frozen river in the middle of winter might not seem like the best way to spend Christmas Day, but Washington assured his soldiers (roughly 5,000 of them) that it would be worth it. He knew that on the other side of the Delaware River in Trenton, New Jersey, about 1,400 German troops (who were helping the British) would be busy celebrating Christmas and definitely not expecting an attack. If they could get past them, they could push east. It was the ideal time to try and turn the war around.

So Washington and his commanders organised the troops into three groups, all planning to cross at different points, but the river was so icy that only one group of about 2,400 soldiers was able to cross. Led by Washington, they used cargo boats, ferries, any vessels they could find, to make the crossing. The weather was truly AWFUL, with freezing rain, snow and high winds, but the soldiers landed on the other side at about 11 p.m. on Christmas Day. They were cold, tired, hungry and three hours behind schedule, but Washington urged them on towards their enemy's fort.

Fortunately, Washington's boldness was rewarded. When his army attacked just after dawn, the British were caught by surprise and surrendered within an hour and a half. So the Battle of Trenton was pretty short and totally ruined Christmas, for one side at least.

This festive victory gave the Continental Army a massive boost and they soon won another battle in Princeton in January 1777. The colonists kept going, but it wasn't until October 1777 that things really began to turn in their favour. After defeating the British in Saratoga, New York, the colonists got a new ally: France. They sent ships and soldiers to help drive the British out of America.

It still took a few more years, though, with both sides winning and losing battles and suffering great hardships. But, in 1781, the British finally surrendered and the war was over. When Britain signed the Treaty of Paris in 1783, it not only officially brought peace, but it also meant that they recognised that the United States of America was an independent country that should rule itself.

WHATEVER HAPPENED TO GEORGE WASHINGTON?

After the American Revolution ended, the United States still had a lot of work to do before it could become a truly unified country. At first all the different states just governed themselves and did what they thought was best for them. They didn't necessarily support each other or work together. It caused quite a few problems.

Fortunately, people realised that things needed to change, so representatives from all the states got together in 1787 and wrote the United States Constitution, which set out the rules for creating a national (federal) government in which the different states shared power and made laws together. States would still have power over some things in their own region, but they would work together on all the important matters. The constitution also set out the rights for individuals in the USA.

> The US Constitution is the oldest written constitution in the world and it is still the foundation of US laws today.

The constitution came into effect in 1789, and the first thing that the new government needed was to elect a president to take overall charge. Representatives from each state put forward their choices for president and the person who got the most votes was . . . George Washington!

So, George Washington, the hero of Christmas Day 1776, became the first-ever president of the USA, and after he died the new US capital city was named after him.

STOCKING FILLER FACTS

CLEVER CHRISTMAS IDEAS

George Washington had a brilliant idea at Christmas that helped to change history. And he's not the only one. In fact, some amazing things have been created on Christmas Day over the years, and not just your granny's famous roast potatoes.

RIGHT ON TIME

On Christmas Day 1656, Dutch astronomer and mathematician Christiaan Huygens came up with a very helpful invention: a pendulum clock. Using a weight known as a pendulum, this clock made keeping time more accurate than ever.

THE SECRET HISTORY OF CHRISTMAS

FINISHED AT LAST

Have you ever started an enormous jigsaw puzzle at Christmas and then given up before finishing it? Well, famous architect Sir Christopher Wren had been working on St Paul's Cathedral for THIRTY-FIVE YEARS and finally, on Christmas Day 1711, Parliament declared that the building was complete. Nice work – now maybe you should go and finish that jigsaw …

IS IT HOT IN HERE?

On Christmas Day 1741, Swedish scientist Anders Celsius transformed the way that people measured temperature. Previous temperature scales were inconsistent, which made it difficult for scientists to get precise data. So, Celsius invented a new scale that went from 0 to 100 degrees and was based on the freezing and boiling points of water. It made a lot of sense and most people measure temperature in this way. The scale is even named after its inventor.

CHAPTER 10

A CHRISTMAS REBELLION

On 25 December 1831, Samuel Sharpe, a Baptist preacher and enslaved person, organised a strike in Jamaica. He encouraged enslaved people to stop working until they were given fair wages and more time off.

He chose Christmas Day because it was a time of celebration and peace. He hoped that people would be in the mood to listen to and give enslaved people the freedom they deserved. Although the rebellion did not go exactly as Samuel Sharpe had planned, it became a key moment on the path to ending slavery.

THE TRANSATLANTIC SLAVE TRADE

As an enslaved person, Samuel Sharpe was not free. He was considered to be owned by someone else and had to do what they said. Often that meant working long hours in harsh conditions and not being paid. Samuel Sharpe was one of millions of Black people who were enslaved at that time.

Slavery had existed for thousands of years – there were enslaved people in ancient Rome and ancient Greece. However, between around 1500 and 1800, at least 15 million people were taken against their will from their homes in Africa and brought across the sea to North and South America, as part of what became known as the transatlantic slave trade. They were bought and sold without their consent and forced to work for the people who owned them.

Enslaved people were often used to produce valuable goods such as cotton, sugar and tobacco. They worked incredibly hard to make other people rich, with little free time or care for their wellbeing. If they had any children, they were automatically enslaved too and the enslavers often used fear and violence to make sure that their enslaved workers did not rebel.

> Enslaved people could only get their freedom if they ran away, if they could somehow 'buy' themselves or if their owner freed them.

NO MORE

It is terrible that slavery was allowed to happen at all, let alone to continue for so long. Eventually people started to call for it to be stopped forever.

By the late eighteenth century, the pressure to end the slave trade was getting stronger. Lots of different people, from politicians and religious leaders to workers and women's groups (who were also campaigning for women's right to vote), all joined the movement to end slavery. This was known as the abolitionist movement. People who had been enslaved also told their stories so others could understand what it was like for them.

In 1807, the slave trade was abolished in Britain and throughout its empire, which meant that people could not be traded any more. But that didn't mean that slavery was abolished completely, so it did not help people like Samuel Sharpe who were already enslaved. Things might have been changing, but for Samuel Sharpe and others, 'might' wasn't good enough.

A CHRISTMAS REBELLION

Sharpe decided he needed to make something happen NOW.

PLANNING A REBELLION

Many enslaved people could not read or write (because they were not allowed to go to school), but Samuel Sharpe could. He read about the abolitionist movement in Britain and it inspired him to take action too. As a Baptist preacher, he was allowed to travel between different estates (properties owned by different enslavers) and hold religious services and meetings. This is how Sharpe was able to spread his secret idea for a peaceful Christmas protest, as he travelled around the island of Jamaica in December 1831.

Lots of people thought it was a good idea and said they would join in. Sharpe emphasised that he wanted their protest to be peaceful. On 25 December 1831, thousands of enslaved people in Jamaica joined Sharpe's rebellion and refused to work. However, the enslavers were not in the mood to make changes or even to listen to what the enslaved people wanted, and they sent soldiers to force everyone to return to work.

With British warships anchored off the coast ready to send in more soldiers, what started as a peaceful protest soon escalated into a full-scale, violent rebellion with up to 60,000 enslaved people fighting back by trying to seize control of properties or setting fire to them. But the rebels were no match for armed soldiers and by 4 January, the Christmas Rebellion was over. The punishments for anyone thought to be involved were brutal, especially for Samuel Sharpe. He lost his life, but he said that he had no regrets for his actions.

1833 SLAVERY ABOLITION ACT

The 1831 Christmas Rebellion did not end slavery, but it helped to bring about its end. Enslavers were worried that there would be more rebellions, while more and more people in Britain were joining the calls to end slavery, especially when they read about the brutal treatment of the Christmas Day rebels in 1831. Things had to change. Finally, in 1833, the British government officially abolished slavery.

Although this was a big step, and many other countries were passing similar laws, in reality little changed for many enslaved people at first. Enslavers received lots of money from the government to compensate them for the loss of their workers, but enslaved people did not, and most of them were still not really free. Many were forced to become 'apprentices' instead and had to keep working long days, with harsh punishments if they didn't. Only after the apprenticeship scheme ended in 1838 were enslaved people actually free to go where they wanted.

SLAVERY IN THE USA

In the USA, slavery did not end until 1865, when the country's constitution was amended to abolish it and free enslaved people. This came at the end of the US Civil War (between northern states, known as the Union, and southern states, known as the Confederacy), in which the issue of slavery had been one of the key points of disagreement. Some states had banned slavery but others were in favour of keeping it. Before slavery came to an end in the US, many enslaved people found clever ways to escape. But this one, at Christmas 1848, was one of the most incredible.

FREEDOM AT CHRISTMAS

Ellen and William Craft were a married couple from Georgia, in the southern USA, who had been enslaved all their lives. They wanted to escape and start a new life in one of the states where slavery was not permitted, so they came up with an audacious plan. Ellen would cut her hair and dress as a male enslaver,

A CHRISTMAS REBELLION

William would pretend to be her slave and they would travel north to freedom. She would hide her face with bandages and wear her arm in a sling to avoid too many questions and having to sign anything. (Neither Ellen nor William could write.)

It was a huge risk and they would have been severely punished if they had been caught, but incredibly, they made it. They set out on 21 December 1848, by train, but had to sit in different carriages due to racial segregation rules. William's enslaver nearly found him at the train station, but he managed to hide. The next stage of their journey involved a steam-powered boat and then after that they had to take another train. They were nearly found out several times, especially when Ellen could not sign her name. Thanks to her bandaged arm and face she managed to get around it, and on

Christmas Day 1848, Ellen and William arrived in Philadelphia, Pennsylvania, where slavery was not allowed. They were free.

CHRISTMAS MAGIC

Christmas is a special time of year when people try to spread joy and love and focus on the best things in life. But Christmas can also be a time for wonder, for change, for taking chances, for daring to dream and for amazing things to happen.

It's no coincidence that so many incredible things have happened on 25 December. The magic of Christmas Day inspires people to believe in the extraordinary and to be bold. Maybe these secret histories and hidden stories of Christmas have inspired you to do something awesome this Christmas and make some history of your own? If not, here's one last stocking filler with some ideas you might want to try . . .

STOCKING FILLER FACTS

CHRISTMAS WORLD RECORDS

Perhaps this Christmas Day could break a festive world record. How about trying to beat one of these?

MINCE PIE EATING

Do you think you could eat three mince pies in a minute? That's the world record – well 52.21 seconds, to be exact. However, if you do try this at home, remember to always EAT RESPONSIBLY.

BUILDING A GINGERBREAD HOUSE

If you like practical challenges, this one could be for you. It would take precise engineering skill as well as speed to beat the world record for building a gingerbread house, which is an incredible 1 minute and 58.26 seconds. At least you can eat it if you fail!

WRAPPING UP A PERSON

Some people love wrapping presents and their gifts look so beautiful that it's almost a shame to unwrap them. Others are not so talented... However, wrapping up a present could be much more fun if it's part of a group challenge. The world record time for eight people to wrap up a human in gift paper is 41.10 seconds. Could your family beat that?

MOST BAUBLES IN A BEARD

The world record, set in December 2022, is 710 baubles in a single beard. Of course, either you need to have a very long beard or you need to find a very patient beard owner. If you don't have enough baubles, you could try candy canes instead. The world record for candy canes in a beard (held by the same person as the baubles!) is 187.

FOR MORE INSPIRING NON-FICTION FROM WREN & ROOK, WHY NOT TRY ...

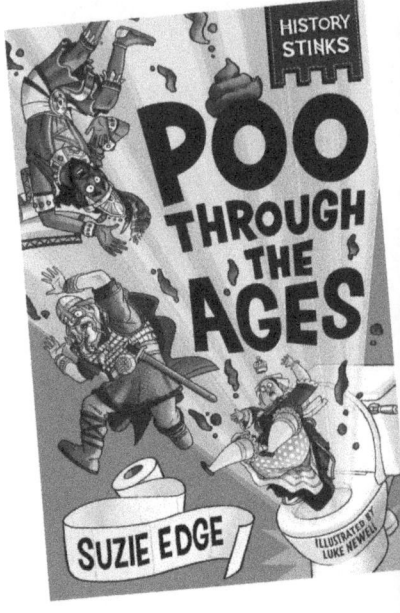
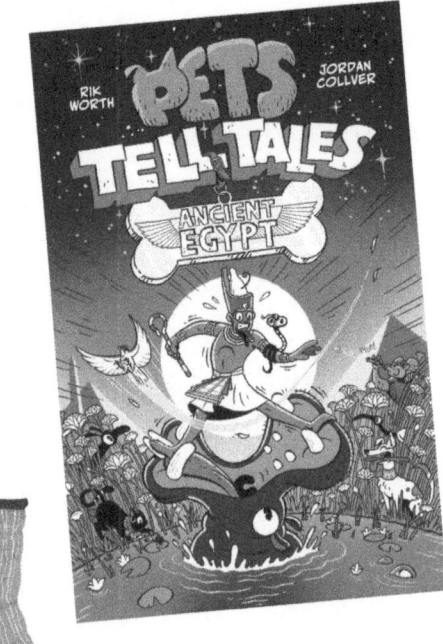

wren & rook